PEARL HARBOR

The Way It Was - December 7, 1941

Text by Scott C.S. Stone

AN ISLAND HERITAGE SPECIAL EDITION

Published by ISLAND HERITAGE
A division of The Madden Corporation

15th printing - 1989
Copyright © 1977 Island Heritage
All rights reserved.

Please address orders
and correspondence to:
Island Heritage
99-880 Iwaena Street
Aiea, Hawaii 96701-3248
(808) 487-7299

Printed and bound in Hong Kong
Library of Congress Number 77-82234 Catalog
ISBN 0-89610-088-X

USS Arizona at sea, 1939.

December 6, 1941, was a lovely, calm day in the Hawaiian Islands. Ashore, the city people of Honolulu, the small-town people and farmers, the beach-dwellers and the beach-goers enjoyed a golden day which melded into a blue evening of crystal stars and soft trade winds. On the ships at Pearl Harbor, especially the big dreadnaughts along Battleship Row, the sailors were relaxed in the easy ambience of life aboard a ship in port. The heart of the Pacific Fleet, the eight magnificent battleships, lay in a line along the gentle reach of Ford Island in the center of Pearl Harbor. From a hill overlooking Pearl Harbor you could see them riding calmly in the water, and see the sailors moving about the decks with easy familiarity. It was a typical warm Saturday on a lush and slow paced island, which also happened to be America's military headquarters in the Pacific. It is likely that no one, afloat or ashore, gave much thought to a rumor which the U.S. Ambassador had picked up in Tokyo almost a year earlier, and which he relayed to the U.S. government. The rumor was that a large and powerful Japanese force would attack Pearl Harbor.

There was a sea like hammered steel and a sky that reached away beyond his comprehension. Each morning since the task force had sailed on November 26, he had made his way to the flight deck to taste the wind-driven salt spray and stare at the trackless ocean and the awesome sky. Nothing in Japan had prepared him for the immensity of it, and it had infected him with a growing sense of his own smallness. He wondered if he were ready for the action to come, for the enormity of the raid that had been so long and so well planned. Each morning he had tried to shake off that suspicion of inadequacy, for he was Masato Katayama, officer and pilot, descendant of samurai warriors. Soon he would hurtle from the deck of the carrier and strike with a searing quickness into the heart of the enemy fleet.

From the deck of the Akagi he felt, but could not see, the ships around him—the Kaga and Soryu and Hiryu, the Zuikaku and Shokaku, all under Vice Admiral Chuichi Nagumo. The gossip was that Nagumo-san was reluctant to carry out this raid, but he was driven by the man who had driven the entire Imperial Navy since 1939, Admiral Isoroku Yamamoto. Everyone knew Yamamoto-san's commitment to the strike; you could see it in the size of the task force, 31 ships, including the carriers and the battleships Hiei and Kirishima. Somewhere out there in that slate-colored pre-dawn sea, five midget submarines were launched from mother submarines, and all around were the destroyers and the support forces.

Yes, he was part of an armada, rehearsed and prepared back in Kagoshima, launched in the bleak morning from Tankan Bay in the Remote Kuriles. He was a part of Japan's destiny, so perhaps not so insignificant after all.

But it was a cold sea and a merciless sky, and as he had done so many times before he turned to the east and searched for a glimpse of the rising sun. At that moment he heard

5

the call he had waited for these many mornings: pilots were to report for the traditional breakfast of rice balls and green tea. As he hurried below he noticed many pilots already wearing the white headband, the hachimaki, which symbolized their willingness to die for Japan. Katayama disdained it; he was a samurai, he had embraced the Bushido code of the warrior and he wore the hachimaki on his soul.

Afterwards, when he had visited the shipboard shrine and made his peace, he waited beside his Zero-sen. He was impassive as he heard the engines sputter to life, but felt a growing tension as Commander Mitsuo Fuchida prepared to lead the first wave from the carrier Akagi. In Japan it was December 8, but on the decks of the task force 230 miles north of Oahu it was December 7, 1941, and it was exactly 6 a.m.

Katayama was startled by the suddenness of the three traditional "banzai" cheers, then he felt something within him move as Fuchida's bomber lumbered from the carrier's deck.

It had begun. He glanced to his left and thought he saw, far out on the horizon, the sun fracturing on the edge of the sea . . . .

Crewmen cheer as aircraft begin taking off for the attack on Pearl Harbor from the pitching decks of carriers. Japanese aviators regarded the attack as a "divine mission" and vowed to make it a crushing blow.

Above: *As the attacking force turns due
south, launch operations begin in the face of
a heavy overcast and a stiff northeast wind.
More than 180 aircraft made up the first
wave to be hurled against U.S. ships, planes
and men on that warm Sunday in December.*

An hour earlier the Japanese had launched two reconnaissance seaplanes from the cruisers Chikuma and Tone, but not even they were the first contact with the enemy force. At 3:45 a.m. the U.S. minesweeper Condor sighted a periscope off the entrance to Honolulu Harbor and notified the destroyer Ward. At 6:30 a.m., the Ward, alert and restless from the first sighting, found a submarine apparently trailing the target ship Antares toward the harbor entrance in an area where no submarine should have been. The Ward opened fire.

The destroyer's second salvo devastated the submarine's conning tower, and set the submarine up for the kill. The Ward raced over and unleashed depth charges, and knew the submarine was doomed. The Ward reported the action to Naval headquarters,

Below: Rolling toward its rendezvous in Hawaiian skies, a Nakajima torpedo bomber begins the lift-off to join the attackers at a point just north of Oahu. The actual launching surpassed previous practice efforts.

where the message took almost an hour to reach the Pacific Fleet Commander-in-Chief, Rear Admiral Husband E. Kimmel. Since submarine sightings had been reported often in the edgy atmosphere of the U.S.-Japanese relations, the Admiral asked for amplification of the message.

Meanwhile, two Army privates in an isolated mobile radar station in the hills near the town of Waialua spotted a lone aircraft. It failed to excite them; they had no way of knowing it was one of the Japanese seaplanes, scouting ahead of the strike aircraft. Soon after that their screen was filled with images, which they correctly identified as waves of aircraft approaching from three degrees east of north. Although it was after their duty shift ended, the two men stayed on and reported the image to an Army lieutenant, who reasoned the planes were a formation of B-17s due to arrive in Hawaii that day from the Mainland. Or, mused the officer,

Left: *Aground and battered by the surf, one of five Japanese midget submarines launched prior to the air strike lies helpless on a windward Oahu beach. The lone survivor of the two-man crew became the first Japanese prisoner of war in combat with America. All of the midget submarines were lost—one beached, two sunk, and two missing at sea.*

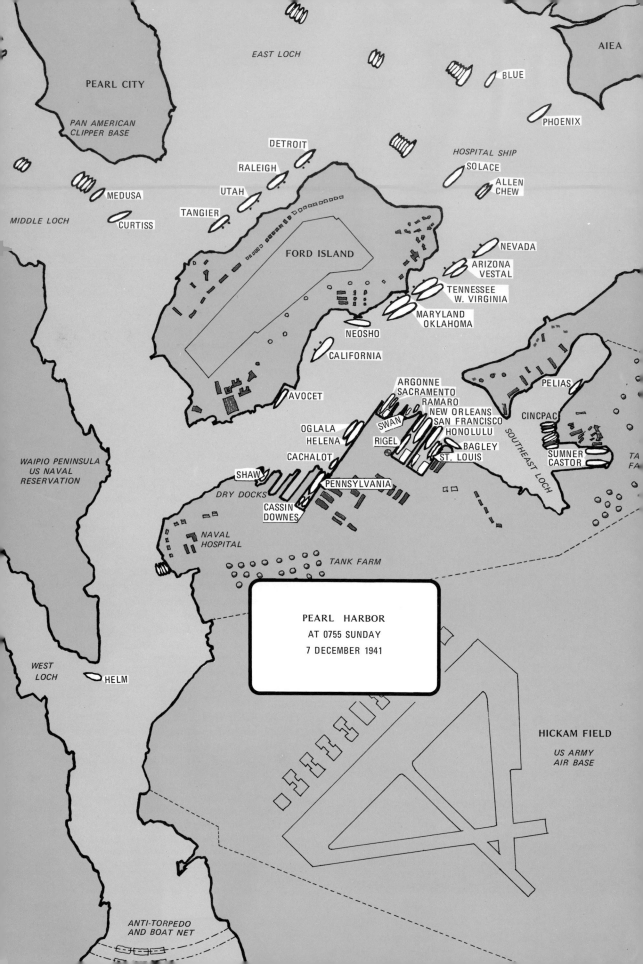

EAST LOCH

AIEA

PEARL CITY

PAN AMERICAN
CLIPPER BASE

BLUE

PHOENIX

HOSPITAL SHIP

DETROIT

SOLACE

RALEIGH

ALLEN
CHEW

MEDUSA

UTAH

MIDDLE LOCH

TANGIER

NEVADA

CURTISS

ARIZONA
VESTAL

FORD ISLAND

TENNESSEE
W. VIRGINIA

MARYLAND
OKLAHOMA

NEOSHO

CALIFORNIA

PELIAS

AVOCET

ARGONNE
SACRAMENTO
RAMARO
NEW ORLEANS
SAN FRANCISCO
HONOLULU

CINCPAC

SWAN

OGLALA
HELENA

RIGEL

BAGLEY
ST. LOUIS

CACHALOT

SUMNER
CASTOR

WAIPIO PENINSULA
US NAVAL
RESERVATION

SHAW

SOUTHEAST LOCH

TA
FA

DRY DOCKS

PENNSYLVANIA

CASSIN
DOWNES

NAVAL
HOSPITAL

TANK FARM

WEST
LOCH

HELM

PEARL HARBOR

AT 0755 SUNDAY

7 DECEMBER 1941

HICKAM FIELD

US ARMY
AIR BASE

ANTI-TORPEDO
AND BOAT NET

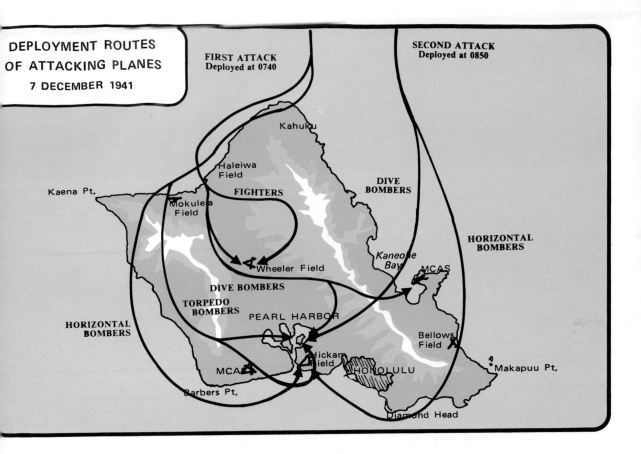

FIRST ATTACK
Deployed at 0740

SECOND ATTACK
Deployed at 0850

Kahuku

DIVE BOMBERS

Haleiwa Field

FIGHTERS

Kaena Pt.

Mokuleia Field

HORIZONTAL BOMBERS

Kaneohe Bay

MCAS

Wheeler Field

DIVE BOMBERS

TORPEDO BOMBERS

PEARL HARBOR

Bellows Field

HORIZONTAL BOMBERS

MCAS

Hickam Field

HONOLULU

Makapuu Pt.

Barbers Pt.

Diamond Head

they might be a carrier aircraft landing ahead of the ship's arrival as was often done. The two privates were still on the line. "Don't worry about it," he told them. It was 7:20 a.m.

An hour and forty minutes after screaming from the carriers' decks, Fuchida's aircraft had deployed over the northern coastline of Oahu, the first of 360 aircraft to be thrown against the sleeping giants waiting just ahead.

Fuchida led a group of 49 bombers carrying 1,600-pound armor-piercing bombs. On his right were 40 Nakajima torpedo-bombers and on his left, each carrying a 500-pound bomb, were more than 50 Aichi dive-bombers.

Above them, in one of the 42 Zeros flying air cover in the event of enemy aircraft attacks, Katayama looked wonderingly at the formation. They hardly looked dangerous at this altitude, but they were the best-trained naval pilots in the world, encased in planes that were splendidly engineered. He stared at them, then took his eyes away to scan the sky around him, but there were no aircraft but

Japanese aircraft in the warm morning sun. Could it be the surprise was going to be as complete as the spies planted on Oahu had promised it would be? The fact that there were no carriers in the harbor was a disappointment, but the latest reports confirmed that the battleships were there, and the battleships were the nucleus of the Pacific Fleet.

Beneath him the bombers swung to the right and passed below in majestic formation, bright as the white dots of sailboats on Lake Biwa. He dipped the right wing slightly for a better look, then straightened it again. He anticipated the thrill of a landfall after so many days of empty ocean.

Ten thousand feet below the formation, Oahu came out of the sea green and glistening, an incredibly beautiful sight in the soft light of the great yellow sun. Katayama saw, with surprise, that the aircraft on the nearest field had been grouped in the center of the field, making them an easy target. He

Left: *Inviting targets—the positions of the Pacific Fleet ships just before the attack.*

Above: *The attack routes for one of history's most devastating surprise raids on a sleeping enemy.*

squinted, trying to see farther, quicker. No smoke came from the ships in the harbor, so none of them had managed to get underway. Even from that great height it was easy to see the surprise was total, and fatal. It was going to be a glorious victory, and his heart leaped with the thought of his role in it. Then he saw a flare come from the direction of Fuchida-san's bomber. It was the order to attack.

The dive-bombers climbed to 15,000 feet and split into two graceful, arching groups. Katayama watched them with pride in their skill as one group headed for Ford Island in the center of Pearl Harbor, the other shot like an arrow at Wheeler Field northwest of the harbor. The torpedo-bombers, meanwhile, sliced downward near the surface of the sea and began their approach. Fuchida-san's radio operator tapped out a pre-arranged signal, "To-To-To . . .," the alert that the first wave had been committed. Moments later came a second signal, the longed-for message that surprise was complete. It was the Japanese word for tiger, repeated and repeated, "Tora . . . Tora . . . Tora . . ."

●

In the harbor along the southwest side of Ford Island the mammoth gray ships lay in the calm of a sun-drenched Sunday. There was the battleship California, moored alone; the battleships Maryland and Oklahoma, with the Maryland moored inboard; the battleships Tennessee and West Virginia, with the West Virginia outboard; the battleship Arizona, moored inboard of the repair ship Vestal; and directly behind the Arizona, the battleship Nevada. Eight of the nine battleships in the Pacific Fleet were enjoying a quiet day of rest. The eighth, the Pennsylvania, was across the harbor from Battleship Row, resting easily in Drydock One at the Navy Yard.

In the repair basin were two 10,000-ton cruisers, the New Orleans and San Francisco. Also in the harbor were four 10,000-ton cruisers; the Phoenix was moored north of Ford Island, and the St. Louis, Honolulu and Helena were in docks at the Navy Yard.

Two 7,000-ton cruisers, the Raleigh and the Detroit, were moored northwest of Ford

Left: *Ford Island, in the center of Pearl Harbor, as the holocaust begins. This photo, from Japanese sources, was taken in the opening moments of the air strike.*

Island. To the north and west of the island were 29 destroyers, considered new. Twenty-six of them had been built since 1933.

In various slots around the harbor were five submarines, a gunboat, 11 minesweepers, 23 auxiliary ships, nine minelayers, and a scattering of smaller craft—a total of 96 ships.

But very little was stirring aboard the ships. On the Tennessee a mess cook stood sipping coffee and enjoying a morning even more lovely than most. On the Arizona a boatswain's mate was standing at the railing, staring down at the paintwork along the hull. Crewmen on various ships were easing their way topside in the soft glow of morning, preparing to hoist colors on the fantails of the warships. A small boat was pushing off from the Merry Point landing, a toy boat on a sheltered sea.

On Ford Island a seaman stood idly watching the sun glittering on the calm harbor waters. On the Oklahoma the forenoon watch had been piped to breakfast, and on several of the ships the gun crews being relieved of watch were wiping dew from the anti-aircraft batteries. The morning was so quiet the sound of church bells echoed gently, signaling the 8 o'clock mass.

It was 7:55 a.m., a moment Katayama knew he would remember all his life.

"Banzai," he whispered, and it grew into a great shout of joy, "banzai . . . banzai!"

The dive-bombers swarmed across Ford Island in a rite of mechanical savagery, loosing their bombs on the aircraft and hangars be-

Below: *On its deadly mission, a dive bomber hurtles toward its victims, neatly aligned along Battleship Row.*

Bottom: *Ex-battleship Utah lists heavily from two direct torpedo hits. She later capsized, trapping many below decks.*

low. Katayama saw the airplanes on the ground flash apart and start to burn—the first smoke of an incendiary morning. Riveted by the destruction, he forced himself to swing the Zero around and search the sky, but he saw no danger. Then he turned back just in time to see the torpedo-bombers skimming 100 feet above the waters of Pearl Harbor, aiming for the long gray targets moored helplessly along Battleship Row.

As Katayama watched, torpedoes, fitted with wooden fins for shallow running in the sheltered waters, cut through the surface and began their deadly run while the pilots jerked their Nakajimas toward the security of the high skies. Katayama saw the flickering of guns aboard the ships; the Americans had come alive.

Then the harbor rocked with explosions and smoke roiled into the clear morning air. Katayama stopped trying to count the hits; he only knew that the battleships suddenly were blazing and that the dense smoke spiraled up and up, dark banners that signaled the death of the ships.

The Oklahoma took three torpedoes and began to list, smoke pouring out of her.

The Arizona shuddered and heaved with the devastation of a bomb in the forward powder magazine. A sudden and intense fire boiled out of the heart of the ship, and her decks were hidden by great, roiling clouds of choking smoke.

The West Virginia took torpedoes and two heavy bombs, igniting a fire amidships.

A torpedo passed beneath the minelayer Oglala and slammed into the cruiser Helena, and exploded. Then a bomb fell between the two ships and went off with a roar.

A torpedo smashed into the cruiser Raleigh and two others streaked into the side of the Utah, formerly a battleship and now an American target vessel. The Utah began an ominous list to port and men leaped from her decks, only to be strafed in the water by passing Japanese aircraft.

Still the planes kept coming.

The Arizona took five torpedoes and a

Below: *Skimming almost at sea level, the torpedo bombers launch projectiles designed to run shallow in the sheltered harbor waters.*

Below: *Writing from the explosions of bombs and torpedoes, the giant battleships, heart of the Pacific Fleet, burn at their moorings, sending billows of black smoke into the clear morning skies over Oahu.*

number of aerial bombs; the armor-piercing bomb which detonated in the forward magazine also set off the Arizona's main forward battery and dropped two gun turrets and the ship's conning tower 20 feet below their natural positions. There was a tremendous amount of oil in the water around the ship, and it burned for hours.

Two more torpedoes hammered the Oklahoma, even as she capsized. Men were running along the canting hull.

In drydock, the Pennsylvania jolted from a bomb blast.

The West Virginia buckled under the force of two bombs, then lurched from the tearing impact of six torpedoes. She began to settle in the water, her main deck just above the harbor's surface.

The Tennessee, moored inboard and escaping the torpedoes, was hit by bombs that threw debris at dangerous random about her decks . . . .

Katayama looked down in amazement on a scene of destruction that seemed so total, so final, that it was almost beyond his grasp. The West Virginia was sinking. The California was settling at the stern. The Oklahoma was capsizing, and the Arizona was in ruins. They were more than names on a chart to him now.

He could see oil gushing from some of the ships and the flames spreading on the water. He thought he could see small boats, probably bent on rescue work, but then his squadron went into a banking turn again, and he remembered his mission—but again there were no enemy aircraft, only the incredibly pure sky and the great, stately clouds. And, as he nosed down again, the black and billowing smoke.

Out of his vision but simultaneous with the

Left: *In slashing attacks, Japanese aircraft bomb and strafe Wheeler Field and other air bases on Oahu, where planes had been grouped to thwart possible saboteurs.*

Above: *High-level bomber looses its package of destruction. Some 50 Nakajimas were equipped to carry heavy bombs instead of torpedoes.*

Below: *Wheeler Field is racked with bomb blasts, ending the defenders' hopes of getting interceptors into action.*

Right: *A ship's magazine explodes after direct hits from the attacking aircraft.*

Following Page: *On Ford Island, the Naval Air Station is sewn with destruction and a fireball suddenly leaps into the darkening sky.*

attack on Battleship Row, bombers and fighters were screaming over Oahu's airfields, scattering death. At Schofield Barracks in north-central Oahu, fighters tore through the mountain pass and raked the compounds and the drill fields with deadly fire. At Hickam Field, near Pearl Harbor, men leaped for cover as bombs tore into shops and buildings, and into the aircraft drawn up in neat rows.

At Wheeler Field the fifty-odd U.S. fighter planes were grouped neatly in front of their hangars. The P-36s and P-40s glinted in the morning sunlight, immobile with surprise as the dive-bombers curved downward and began their runs, with a group of Zeros close behind.

The fighters on the ground wrenched apart with the impact of the bombs, sending fiery pieces of debris into the air. Some airplanes simply vanished in the force of the explosions. Men crossing the runways were caught and killed by the spinning debris and by Japanese strafing planes which came hard out of the sun. Hangars burst apart in the fury of the attack. More than 40 of the combat planes on the ground flamed and burned; others were badly damaged and never got into the air.

At Kaneohe, on the windward side of Oahu, the Naval Air Station was strafed twice, then bombed. Of the 33 planes on the ground, 27 were smashed and burned, some bent beyond recognition. Smoke from burning planes reached high over the sleepy windward side and disappeared in wisps, like black cirrus against the morning light.

Around Ford Island, the scene was one of havoc.

Men swam about in the water, trying to escape the holocaust. Burning oil covered the surface, a malevolent film with flames licking from it. The air was heavy and hard to breathe. Staccato gunfire mingled with the sounds of screams and curses.

A wave of dive-bombers came in low and fast and struck at the Maryland and the Nevada and various light cruisers and destroyers.

One destroyer, the Monaghan, got underway and headed for the harbor entrance. But west of Ford Island the ship spotted a Japanese submarine under attack by the Curtiss and Tangier. The Curtiss had hit the submarine's conning tower but the Monaghan's actions were quick and direct—she rammed the submarine, then crossed it with depth charges, and saw the water turn dark with oil. Finally, followed now by the destroyer Henley, the Monaghan sped toward the relative safety of the open ocean.

Overhead, eight groups of high-altitude bombers began weaving a cruel pattern, crossing the harbor in precise checkerboard formations.

The battleship Nevada managed to get underway, the only ship of her class to do so that morning. Hit in the forward section by a torpedo, she plowed uncertainly into the channel waters and headed for sea. At the southwestern point of Ford Island the ship rocked with the sudden and brutal smash of bombs. Her deck was dotted with gaping holes and her superstructure was flaming. Could she reach the channel entrance and make it through to safety, or would she sink

Left: *The battleship Nevada, only ship of her class to get underway during the attack, deliberately runs aground to avoid the possibility of sinking and blocking the channel entrance.*

Below: *Captured Japanese film shows the burning ships along Battleship Row.*

Right: *The battleships were prime targets for swarming enemy attackers, who found all but one of the Pacific Fleet's dreadnoughts in the harbor. The USS Colorado was being repaired in Bremerton, Washington, at the time of the attack.*

at the mouth and block the entrance for the other ships? Fourteenth Naval District officers decided not to risk it and the Nevada was ordered aground. She turned shoreward and ran her proud hull onto the point of land near the channel mouth.

Alongside the dying Arizona, the repair ship Vestal managed to get free and anchor again northeast of Ford Island. The Oglala, moved by tugs to a more secure position, suddenly capsized. The Neosho, filled with high-octane aviation gas, managed to clear herself and stand away from the flames . . . .

Right: *Anti-aircraft fire crackles above Pearl Harbor. The Japanese attack commander credited gun crews on the ships with recovering from the surprise quicker than Imperial Navy sailors could have done, and some of the return fire was deadly.*

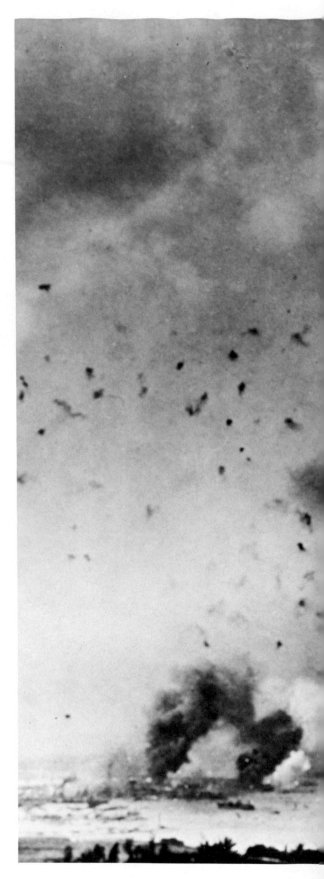

Katayama was growing restless. It was obvious that no enemy aircraft were going to threaten the attacking planes, and he decided now to go to his secondary mission. He looked about him and saw his wingman staring back; perhaps he was having the same thoughts. Katayama clenched his fist and turned it thumbs down and saw the wingman nod.

As he nosed down toward the tapestry of death and destruction below, he was suddenly aware of the black flowers of anti-aircraft fire opening up nearer and nearer. He threw the Zero around in a violent shift to the right, dropped it expertly and turned back to the left to line up for his strafing run.

The Zero screamed down and down. Katayama felt his heart pounding wildly and he fought to stay calm. He picked a dock where he saw men running, and he leveled the Zero and took it low and opened up with his .25 caliber machine guns.

It happened very quickly. One minute they were in his sights and running in panic, and just as suddenly he was over them and pulling up and away, and all the while conscious of a feeling of power such as he had never known in his most vivid fantasies. He grinned. The next run, he would be calmer and more professional.

Still climbing, he saw a puff of smoke off his left wingtip, and all at once, with a rush and a sound like a hurtling train, the black flower bloomed in front of him, tossing the Zero-sen wildly to the right.

He fought the controls instinctively. All at once he became conscious of the shattered canopy in front of him, of a strange whistling noise, and then, deep in his chest, of the first stirrings of an unspeakable pain . . . .

Agony twisted the faces of the men in the water.

Oil-smeared, some more dead than alive, sailors from the stricken Oklahoma clambered onto the hull of the overturned battleship while others slid off into the grimy waters alongside.

From the California, blazing furiously, crewmen slipped into small boats or risked the water itself, even as more oil from the Arizona began to engulf the California's stern.

Small boats converged on the burning ships, but in their wake came the Aichi bombers, stitching the water in deadly strafing runs that shattered boats and bodies. More than two dozen of them in taut formation bore down on the hapless men in the water, and flung themselves against the return fire of the working guns on the crippled ships.

One of the Japanese aircraft began to smoke as it climbed. It leveled at a few hundred feet and began a long, elliptical circle, and suddenly exploded.

Right: *That most dreaded of commands at sea rang through the California soon after the attack began, and sailors obediently began to abandon ship. Rescue operations already were getting underway.*

On the Raleigh a small miracle was taking place. None of the cruiser's crew was dead and only a few wounded. An armor-piercing bomb passed through the ship, ripping up the deck in front of a startled engineer, and blew up in the mud beneath the cruiser. Hit in the port side by a torpedo, the ship managed to stay afloat and her gunners poured round after round into the attacking Aichis. When one of them came apart in a violent explosion, the Raleigh's gun crews cheered.

In the drydocks the destroyers Cassin and Downes exploded like roman candles while firefighters fought the flames in spite of the strafing runs and the danger of ricocheting bullets.

The destroyer Shaw, hit forward by a heavy bomb, blew up with a spectacular burst that flung bodies into the water and scattered debris in all directions. The bomb had exploded all the magazines and tore away the ship's bow.

On the windward side of the island, at Bellows Field, one of the five midget submarines ran aground and the lone survivor struggled ashore, to be captured almost immediately. With midget subs sunk by the Ward and Monaghan and two others lost at sea, the beached submarine was the last of the five launched long before the Japanese aircraft began their attack.

At the Ford Island Naval Air Station a hangar burst with fire and sent long streaks of flame shooting skyward and disappearing to be replaced with other streaks of fire . . . .

Right: *With a roar and a flash of fire, the destroyer Shaw erupts from bombs that blow away the ship's bow. The Shaw was in a floating drydock when the bombs hit.*

The Arizona went down, writhing in death, dying with more than 1,100 men trapped in her hull.

The Oklahoma died on her side, sinking with more than 400 men entombed below her decks.

The California sank like a wounded mammoth, going down at the stern.

The West Virginia settled into the mud of the harbor bottom, her main deck awash in the oil-shrouded water.

The Nevada lay aground, smouldering and shaken with explosions.

Blazing like a gigantic candle, the Utah slipped beneath the surface and disappeared.

The Pennsylvania, Maryland and Tennessee hunched like great wounded beasts, fighting the destruction that threatened them all.

At Wheeler Field, at Hickam, at Kaneohe and Ewa and Ford Island airstrips, the crumpled forms of shattered airplanes were consumed in the flames that leaped from aircraft to aircraft. Everywhere, there was the shape of death and the scent of murder. Bodies lay on aprons and taxiways and runways of the airfields, or rolled in the disturbed waters of the once-sheltering lochs. Huge fires sucked oxygen out of the morning.

And still the Japanese aircraft poured out of the sky, too numerous to count, bringing death to the already dying. The plaintive wail of the sirens, echoing as the church bells had echoed an hour before, came steadily across the water and died in the thunder of detonations and the churning, crackling sound of the killing flames.

For long moments the pain had clawed at him like a trapped beast, and he had fought for consciousness. Now there was still pain, but it was a dull, persistent, numbing hurt, and it frightened him as much as the lacing pain had shocked him.

Katayama eased back on the throttle and looked around the cockpit. At least half the dials were smashed, and the shards of the

Left: *A fireboat
pours water onto the
flaming West
Virginia, which sank
at her moorings at
Ford Island. The
ship's captain was
among those killed
by the attacking
airplanes.*

canopy were everywhere.

His head was heavy, heavy, and his hands moved slowly over the controls. The compass was destroyed and the altimeter smashed. He had no idea how much fuel was left, and he tried to remember the gauge before the explosion, but it seemed such a long time ago.

He knew he had drifted; there was a battle back there, somewhere, but he was no longer a part of it, and it no longer mattered. And he was tired. If he could sleep, the pain might go away . . . .

He snapped his head up again to find the Zero screaming downward, and he forced it back in a panic, taking it up again against the hammer of the wind, feeling the metal flex and strain.

Then he was up and level. He fought down a sudden rush of nausea, and tried to clear his head. He knew he had to stay awake.

●

First reports of damage in the city began reaching Honolulu police shortly after 8 a.m., and increased with the passing minutes.

A building supply house was hit and thousands of dollars in building supplies exploded and burned. A woman was killed in upper Nuuanu Valley. At Lunalilo School the roof suddenly began to blaze and a make-shift first aid station was hurriedly set up on the school grounds to handle casualties.

Japanese strafing planes cut across the roads leading to Pearl Harbor and shot at both cars and pedestrians. At Hickam Field, three civilian firemen were killed and seven hurt while battling a swift-spreading fire.

Several people died when a lunch stand was hit at the corner of Nuuanu and Kukui Streets. At King and McCully Streets, a whole block of buildings was threatened by fire and dozens of families fled into the streets. In the Iwilei district, a large gas tank flamed for a time, and hours after the fire was thought to be out, suddenly flashed again with a bright and glittering flame.

Through the noise and confusion, through the horror and disbelief, the lament of the sirens grated on nerves already raw. Time after time the Honolulu Fire Department joined in fiery combat with the spreading flames. Fire departments on the military bases were either in constant action, or out of action entirely. Sugar plantation firemen near Pearl Harbor fought cane fires ignited by exploding shells.

In the town of Waipahu a shell crashed through the roof of a store, while a nearby hospital was taking four hits. A Japanese aircraft pinwheeled into a pineapple field near Wahiawa town and started a fire which destroyed five homes.

"This is no maneuver . . . this is the real McCoy!" an announcer shouted into his microphone. The destruction around the island and the towers of smoke from the direction of the military bases underscored his warning.

The destruction went on . . . .

A wall was knocked down at Kamehameha School. A shell detonated near the driveway of the Governor's home on Beretania Street in downtown Honolulu. The explosion sent shrapnel slicing through the foliage to kill a pedestrian across the street. Four men were killed in one car while trying to get to Pearl Harbor to help rescue workers.

In a brief lull—hardly more than a decrease in intensity between waves of attackers—a few American aircraft got into the air and shot down several Japanese planes.

Meanwhile, the B-17s, expected earlier, finally arrived in Hawaii to be greeted by a scene of chaos and confusion—and by a swarm of Zeros. In one of the miracles of the day, all 18 of them managed to land safely at one airfield or another.

Eighteen dive-bombers from the carrier Enterprise also arrived over Pearl Harbor at the height of the attack and started drawing fire from friend and enemy alike. A commander landed his plane on Ford Island with smoke billowing upward from a hangar, and American bullet holes in both wings.

Thirteen of the 18 Enterprise aircraft landed at Kaneohe Naval Air Station, but only nine were undamaged. Those nine refueled, took on 500-pound bombs, and went searching for the Japanese Fleet.

The pain and the wind and the eerie whistling of the wind in the smashed canopy had become one awesome force tearing at his consciousness, and with great effort he tried to concentrate on the single thought he was able to hold: find the Akagi.

He had put the sun on his right wing and headed the Zero-sen toward the north. No one could help him now but himself. There was the radio but silence had been ordered, and he knew a call to the carrier would bring no response. At some point the last ounce of fuel would burn and the plane would plummet into that immense ocean, unless he found the task force and took the plane down gently to the haven of the carrier's flight deck.

Find the Akagi. He felt himself growing colder, but still he fought to keep the thought alive. But it was a vast ocean, and an eternal sky. He shook his head; find the Akagi.

●

Vice Admiral Nagumo had moved the task force 40 miles closer, knowing that a few miles could make a large difference to pilots trying to get back to the haven of the decks. By 9:45 a.m. the last Japanese aircraft—it was Commander Fuchida's—had abandoned the terrible skies over Oahu and was en route to the waiting fleet. The weather was worsening and seas were running high.

The admiral was anxious to set course for the Japanese homeland. Preceding the attack, even during it, he had feared some kind of swift retaliation by the American forces, but he was slowly accepting the realization that

he had delivered a crippling blow, that there would be no furious retaliation that might endanger his ships and men.

By 10 a.m., and for the following two hours, the planes were streaming back to the carriers. Two bombers radioed they were lost and asked for a navigation fix, but Nagumo had ordered a strict wireless silence, and the planes disappeared. Jubilant crewmen stood on the carriers' decks, counting the returning aircraft, more than they expected.

On the Akagi, Fuchida had made his report. It was succinct and ended with a recommendation: "Another attack." But the cautious Nagumo had made up his mind. Announcing that "anticipated results have been

Below: *Hulks of once-proud battleships, the Tennessee and West Virginia are masses of twisted steel shortly after the attack began.*

41

achieved," he ran up a signal flag on Akagi's masthead. It was the order for the task force to turn north and run for home.

Katayama had lost track of time.

Along with the wind-noise and the occasional thumping from somewhere deep within the Zero-sen, he could hear his own breathing, harsh and labored. His flight suit felt stiff and wet, and he was bitter cold in the soft sunlight. There was a taste in his mouth, like copper.

The aircraft was a part of him and he of it, the metal skin his skin, the engine noise a counter-point to his own shuddering heart. He knew his mind had wandered, because there was something important he had to do, or remember. But it was easier to put his head back and look at the sky.

With a great effort he turned his head slightly to see the rising sun on the Zero's wingtip. It shone deep and clear and red as blood in the sunlit morning. Katayama straightened his head again and sighed.

The Zero flew on and on until, finally, it began a long and gradual descent toward the sea.

Left: *From across a Pearl Harbor loch, the smoke rising from Ford Island is dramatic evidence of the destruction beneath it.*

Left: *The Arizona, three days later.*

Below: *The remains of a B-17C bomber lie where it was hit at Hickam Field.*

AFTERMATH

In December, 1941, American naval strategy still placed the battleship at the center of the task forces. The aircraft carriers and their ranging airplanes, though in existence, were considered secondary to the battleships in the minds of most naval strategists.

Thus, on December 7, the heart of the Pacific Fleet was nine battleships and three aircraft carriers. Eight of the battleships were in Pearl Harbor that Sunday morning; the ninth, the Colorado, was undergoing work in the Navy Yard at Bremerton, Washington. All of the dreadnoughts were in the 29,000 to 33,000-ton class.

Of the three aircraft carriers assigned to Pearl Harbor, the Saratoga was being repaired on the West Coast. The carrier Enterprise was returning from Wake Island, 2,300 miles to the west (and had sent some aircraft ahead just in time to get caught up in the attack). The carrier Lexington was returning to Pearl Harbor from ferrying aircraft to Midway Island, more than 1,000 miles to the

northwest. Thus, all three escaped attack on that day.

Of the 96 ships in the harbor on December 7, 18 were sunk or heavily damaged.

The Arizona was a total loss, but today is kept sentimentally in commission, and is graced by a memorial to all the war dead of that Sunday morning.

The Oklahoma was a total loss, later raised and sunk again off Oahu to clear the harbor.

The California sank at her berth but was raised and repaired, and took part in the capture of Pacific islands as the U.S. forces neared Japan.

The West Virginia, which also went down at her moorings, was raised, repaired, and still afloat at the end of the war.

The Tennessee was repaired and saw action throughout the Pacific campaign.

The Nevada was refloated, modernized and employed throughout the war. At the time of the attack she was the oldest battleship in the Pacific Fleet. After the war she was a target

Left: *The Oklahoma capsizes after taking five direct hits from shallow-running torpedoes. Her crewmen were strafed as they abandoned ship. Some of the crew scrambled to other ships to assist anti-aircraft batteries.*

ship in the Bikini Atoll bomb tests, later sank under fire from American ships testing other weapons.

The Utah was a total loss, and remains where she sank.

The Pennsylvania was repaired and saw action throughout the war.

The Maryland was repaired and quickly back in action.

The minelayer Oglala was sunk, but salvaged.

The damaged cruisers Helena, Honolulu and Raleigh were repaired and saw action.

The Cassin and Downes, both destroyers in the drydocks, were severely damaged, but the Downes was rebuilt and the Cassin towed to San Francisco and rebuilt there.

The repair ship Vestal and seaplane tender Curtiss were severely damaged, but repaired.

Ninety-two Navy aircraft were destroyed and 31 damaged. The Army Air Corps lost 96 planes and had 128 damaged.

The Navy lost 2,008 officers and men killed, 710 wounded.

The Army had 218 killed, 364 wounded.

The Marines lost 109 killed, with 69 wounded.

There were 68 civilians killed, and 35 wounded.

Total casualties for the day: 2,403 dead, 1,178 wounded.

The attacking Japanese force lost 29 aircraft—15 dive-bombers, five torpedo-bombers and nine fighters. Also lost were the two-
man crews of the five midget submarines,
except for the lone prisoner taken on the
windward side of Oahu.

The advance submarine force also lost a
larger, I-class submarine. The poor showing
of the Japanese submarines was to plague the
Imperial submarine force throughout the
war. It affected later appropriations and
manpower, and the Japanese submariners
had their private, and often bitter, reasons to
remember Pearl Harbor.

Total Japanese casualties: 185 killed, one
captured.

But as the task force steamed toward a
triumphant welcome in Japan after that terrible morning, the Japanese forces had scored
less of a victory than they knew.

They had failed to destroy any American
aircraft carriers, which became the heart of
the rebuilt task forces and turned America
rapidly toward new naval strategies.

They had failed to destroy the repair facilities on Oahu. With those facilities in operation, America was able to salvage and repair
vessels and aircraft which appeared at first to
be destroyed. As part of the United States'
industrial capability, the repair shops helped
put the U.S. forces into the war within days
of the Sunday morning disaster.

The Japanese attack also failed to destroy
the U.S. submarine base or the vengeful U-
boats that soon were at sea in search of Japanese shipping.

In a serious, even fatal, lapse of Intelligence and pre-strike planning, the Japanese
failed to destroy the highly-visible oil storage
tanks. Those tanks soon supplied the fuel for
counter-attacking U.S. ships and aircraft.

For all the carnage of that bloody Sunday,
the Japanese attack was a near-triumph, an
incomplete victory.

Right: *A Japanese midget submarine is
recovered off Oahu nearly 20 years after the
attack. The failure of the submarines on
December 7, 1941, hounded Japanese
submariners throughout the war.*

Below: *For pre-strike planning, Japanese planners used this mock-up of the ships on Battleship Row.*

OPERATION Z

The Japanese plan for the attack on Pearl Harbor was code-named "Operation Z." It was interwoven and inseparable from the events leading up to the surprise attack on Pearl Harbor. Here are some highlights of those events which launched Operation Z:

December, 1940—Admiral Isoroku Yamamoto reveals Operation Z in discussions with his Chief of Staff.

January, 1941—U.S. Ambassador Joseph Grew reports a rumor that the Japanese are planning a surprise attack against Pearl Harbor.

August, 1941—The Japanese propose to make no advances beyond Indo-China if the United States will restore free trade with Japan, discontinue aid to China, and persuade China to recognize Japan's authority in Indo-China.

September, 1941—The Japanese Imperial Conference decides war is necessary if the United States and Japan cannot come to agreements before October.

September, 1941—Spies in the Japanese consulate in Honolulu are ordered to report on U.S. warships in Pearl Harbor.

November, 1941—A "final" Japanese proposal is presented in Washington.

November, 1941—A Japanese task force sails in secret from Tankan Bay in the remote Kurile Islands.

December 1, 1941—The Japanese Privy Council authorizes an attack on Pearl Harbor.

December 2, 1941—The Japanese ambassador in Washington is ordered to destroy all codebooks.

December 7, 1941—At 5:30 a.m., Hawaii time, Washington is alerted to the possibility of attack and warns the Pacific Fleet, a warning which did not arrive in time.

December 7, 1941—At 3:45 a.m., Hawaii time, the USS Condor sights a periscope and makes an alert signal to the destroyer USS Ward.

December 7, 1941—The Japanese unleash a surprise attack on the Pacific Fleet at Pearl Harbor.

Honolulu Star-Bulletin 1st EXTRA

Bulletin Ext. 1902 No. 11278
Star. Vol. XLVIII No. 15356

8 PAGES—HONOLULU, TERRITORY OF HAWAII, U. S. A., SUNDAY, DECEMBER 7, 1941—8 PAGES

★ PRICE FIVE CENTS

WAR !

(Associated Press by Transpacific Telephone)

SAN FRANCISCO, Dec. 7.—President Roosevelt announced this morning that Japanese planes had attacked Manila and Pearl Harbor.

OAHU BOMBED BY JAPANESE PLANES

SIX KNOWN DEAD, 21 INJURED, AT EMERGENCY HOSPITAL

Attack Made On Island's Defense Areas

By UNITED PRESS

WASHINGTON, Dec. 7.—Text of a White House announcement detailing the attack on the Hawaiian islands is:

"The Japanese attacked Pearl Harbor from the air and all naval and military activities on the island of Oahu, principal American base in the Hawaiian islands."

Oahu was attacked at 7:55 this morning by Japanese planes.

The Rising Sun, emblem of Japan, was seen on plane wing tips.

Wave after wave of bombers streamed through the clouded morning sky from the southwest and flung their missiles on a city still sleeping in peaceful Sabbath calm.

According to an unconfirmed report received at the governor's office, the Japanese force that attacked Oahu reached island waters aboard two small airplane carriers.

It was also reported that at the governor's office an attempt had been made to bomb the USS Lexington, or that it had been bombed.

CITY IN UPROAR

Within 10 minutes the city was in an uproar. Bombs fell in many parts of the city, and in some areas the defenders of the islands sprang into quick action.

Army intelligence officers at Ft. Shafter announced officially shortly after 9 a. m. the start of the bombardment by an enemy but that a previous army and navy had taken immediate measures in defense.

"Oahu is under a sporadic air raid," the announcement said.

"Civilians are ordered to stay off the streets until further notice."

CIVILIANS ORDERED OFF STREETS

The army has ordered that all civilians stay off the streets and highways and not use telephones.

Evidence that the Japanese attack has registered some hits was shown by three billowing pillars of smoke in the Pearl Harbor and Hickam field area.

All navy personnel and civilian defense workers, with the exception of women, have been ordered to duty at Pearl Harbor.

The Pearl Harbor highway was immediately a mass of racing cars.

A trickling stream of injured people began pouring into the city emergency hospital a few minutes after the bombardment started.

Thousands of telephone calls almost swamped the Mutual Telephone Co., which put extra operators on duty.

At The Star-Bulletin office the phone calls deluged the single operator and it was impossible for this newspaper, for sometime, to handle the flood of calls. Here also an emergency operator was called.

HOUR OF ATTACK—7:55 A. M.

An official army report from department headquarters, made public shortly before 11, is that the first attack was at 7:55 a. m.

Witnesses said they saw at least 50 airplanes over Pearl Harbor.

The attack centered in the Pearl Harbor, Army authorities said:

"The rising sun was seen on the wing tips of the airplanes."

Although martial law has not been declared officially, the city of Honolulu was operating under M-Day conditions.

It is reliably reported that enemy objectives under attack were Wheeler field, Hickam field, Kaneohe bay and naval air station and Pearl Harbor.

Some enemy planes were reported shot down.

The body of the pilot was seen in a plane burning at Wahiawa.

Oahu appeared to be taking calmly after the first uproar of queries.

ANTIAIRCRAFT GUNS IN ACTION

First indication of the raid came shortly before 8 this morning when antiaircraft guns around Pearl Harbor began sending up a thunderous barrage.

At the same time a vast cloud of black smoke arose from the naval base and also from Hickam field where flames could be seen.

BOMB NEAR GOVERNOR'S MANSION

Shortly before 9:30 a bomb fell near Washington Place, the residence of the governor. Governor Poindexter and Secretary Charles M. Hite were there.

It was reported that the bomb killed an unidentified Chinese man across the street in front of the Schuman Carriage Co. where windows were broken.

C. E. Daniels, a welder, found a fragment of shell or bomb at South and Queen Sts. which he brought into the City Hall. This fragment weighed about a pound.

At 10:05 a. m. today Governor Poindexter telephoned to The Star-Bulletin announcing he has declared a state of emergency for the entire territory.

He announced that Edouard L. Doty, executive secretary of the major disaster council, has been appointed director under the M-Day law's provisions.

Governor Poindexter urged all residents of Honolulu to remain off the street, and the people of the territory to remain calm.

Mr. Doty reported that all major disaster council wardens and medical units were on duty within a half hour of the time the alarm was given.

Workers employed at Pearl Harbor were ordered at 10:10 a. m. not to report at Pearl Harbor.

The mayor's major disaster council was to meet at the city hall at about 10:30 this morning.

At least two Japanese planes were reported at Hawaiian department headquarters to have been shot down.

One of the planes was shot down at Ft. Kamehameha and the other back of the Waterfront.

Hundreds See City Bombed

Hundreds of Honolulans who hurried to the top of Punchbowl soon after bombs began to fall, saw spread out before them the whole panorama of surprise attack and defense.

Far off over Pearl Harbor the white sky was polka-dotted with anti-aircraft smoke.

Rolling away from the navy base were billowing clouds of ugly black smoke. Sometimes a burst of flame reddened the black sources of the smoke.

Out from the silver-surfaced mouth of the harbor a flotilla of destroyers streamed to battle, smoke pouring from their stacks.

Names of Dead and Injured

The city emergency hospital reported at 10:30 a list of 6 killed and 11 injured.

The complete list will be carried later. Here is a partial list:

Prior Lopes, 34, of 3641 Kanaunahi St., was reported at 9:30 a. m. to be in serious condition from wounds in the upper abdomen.

Bernice Gonsvia, 12, 3766 Kaihi St. is suffering from a mangled thigh, lacerations on the right leg and left arm.

A Portuguese girl, unidentified, 10 years old, died on arrival from puncture wounds.

Another victim who died on arrival was Frank Ohaahi, 10, 2706 Kamanaiki St. from puncture wounds in the chest.

Cecilia Brandly, 32, Mountain gardens was released from the hospital after treatment for lacerations.

Three were reported injured and one reported killed from the bomb that fell at Fort and School Sts.

Schools Closed

All schools on Oahu, both public and private, will remain closed until further notice, Edouard L. Doty, territorial director of civilian defense, announced at 11 a. m. today. This does not apply elsewhere in the territory.

Editorial

HAWAII MEETS THE CRISIS

Honolulu and Hawaii will meet the emergency of war today as Honolulu and Hawaii have met emergencies in the past—coolly, calmly and with complete support of the officials, officers and troops who are in charge.

Governor Poindexter and the army and navy leaders have called upon the public to remain calm; for civilians who have no essential business on the streets to stay off; and for every man and woman to do his duty.

That request, coupled with the measures promptly taken to meet the situation that has suddenly and terribly developed, will be needed.

Hawaii will do its part as a loyal American territory.

In this crisis, every difference of race, creed and color will be submerged in the one desire and determination to play the part that Americans always play in crisis.

BULLETIN

Additional Star-Bulletin extras today will cover the latest developments in this war move.

THE ATTACKING WARPLANES

The use of the aircraft carrier and the long reach of its warplanes had developed rapidly through the years following World War I, and its proponents knew the potential of a seaborne aerial strike force. It was a difficult concept, however, for surface admirals to accept. The Japanese attack on Pearl Harbor had an overnight effect. With the destruction or damage of the battleships at Pearl Harbor, the American Navy was forced to perfect the carrier task force, making it the nucleus of the new Pacific Fleet and employing it with great skill throughout World War II.

The Japanese carrier-based warplanes which came from the sea to hammer at the U.S. Fleet and shore installations were skillfully operated and well engineered and tested. The Aichi D3A1 "Val" dive bomber compiled a bomb-hitting accuracy score of 80 percent through the first years of the war, and became formidable dogfighters after their bombs had been released. The Mitsubishi Zero-sen fighter was superior to almost everything else in the skies in 1941, and the Japanese began to believe it was invincible. Allied fighter development caught up with the "Zeke" but not until later in the war.

The Nakajima B5N (Type 97), nicknamed "Kate" was an advanced, even bold, design when it went into production in the early 1930s. By the time of the Pearl Harbor attack the torpedo bomber was evolving into an even better aircraft. Forty of the new B5N2 "Kates" used against the Pacific Fleet at Pearl Harbor had an enviable accuracy rating of at least 50 percent.

Aichi D3AI Model II (Code name "Val" by Allies)

A two-seat, carrier-based dive bomber, the "Val" was powered by a 1,000 horsepower Mitsubishi MK8 Kinsei 44 engine. The "Val" had a ceiling of 31,200 feet and a speed of 242 miles per hour at 7,500 feet. Her empty weight was 5,309 lbs. and at her full loaded weight of 8,041 lbs. the plane had a range of 1,130 miles. Wingspan: 47 feet 1 inch. Length: 33 feet 5 inches. Armament: Two 7.7 mm forward firing machine guns plus up to 700 lbs. of bombs.

Nakajima B5N2 (Code name "Kate" by Allies)

Powered by a 1,000 horsepower Nakajima Sakae II engine, the "Kate" could climb, fully loaded, to 10,000 feet in under eight minutes. With a speed at 10,000 feet of 235 miles per hour, the plane had a ceiling in excess of 25,000 feet and a normal range of 634 miles. Overloaded, range extended to over 1,200 miles. Empty weight 4,830 lbs. Weight when loaded, 8,360 lbs. Wing span: 50 feet 11 inches. Length: 33 feet 10 inches. Armament: One flexible 7.7 mm machine gun in rear cockpit and either one 1,764 lb. torpedo or three 551 lb. bombs.

Mitsubishi A6M2 Zero-sen (Code name "Zeke" by Allies)

With a wingspan of 39 feet 4 inches and a length of 29 feet 9 inches, the Zero was powered by a 940 horsepower Nakajima Sakae engine. Able to climb at nearly 3,000 feet per minute to 20,000 feet, the "Zeke" had a top ceiling of 32,810 feet and a range of 1,160 miles. Top speed was 335 miles per hour. Armament: Two 7.7 mm forward mounted machine guns, two 20 mm Mark 3 cannon, and two 132 lb. bombs.

A MEMORIAL TRIBUTE

Below are names of the heroic men of the USS Arizona who died in action or are presumed dead in the sinking of this great battleship.

The names listed here are a memorial to the memory of all who died in the attack on the morning of December 7, 1941.

NAVAL OFFICERS

Killed in Action
ANDERSON, Lawrence D.

Declared Dead
BARNES, Delmar H.
BATES, Edw. M. Jr.
BOOTH, Robert S. Jr.
BROOKS, Robert N.
CARTER, Paxton T.
CLOUES, Edw. B.
COLE, David L.
CROWLEY, Thomas E.
EMERY, Jack M.
EVANS, Evan F.
FRENCH, John E.
GAZECKI, Philip R.
GOSSELIN, Edward W.
HALLORAN, Wm. I.
HAVERFIELD, James W.
HOLLIS, Ralph
JANZ, Clifford T.
JOHNSON, Samuel E.
JONES, Thomas R.
KIDD, Isaac C.
KING, Robert N. Jr.
KIRKPATRICK, Thomas L.
LAKE, John E. Jr.
LEOPOLD, Robert L.
LOMAX, Frank S.
MANLOVE, Arthur C.
MARSH, Benjamin R. Jr.
McCLUNG, Harvey M.
MERRILL, Howard D.
NOWOSACKI, T.L.
OLSEN, Edw. K.
O'NEILL, Wm. T. Jr.
REGISTER, Paul J.
SANDERS, Eugene T.
SAVAGE, Walter S. Jr.
SMITH, Albert J.
SMITH, Orville S.
UHRENHOLDT, Andrew C.
VAN VALKENBURGH, Franklin
WEEDEN, Carl
WHITEHEAD, Ulmont I. Jr.
WILLIAMS, Laurence A.
WILSON, Neil M.
WINTER, Edw.
WOLF, Geo. A. Jr.
YOUNG, Eric R.

NAVAL ENLISTED MEN

Killed in Action

APREA, Frank Anthony
AUSTIN, Laverne Alfred
AYERS, Dee Cumpie
BAKER, R.D.
BECK, George Richard
BROWN, Richard Corbett
CLEMMENS, Claude Albert
COX, Gerald Clinton
CRISWELL, Wilfred John
DAY, William John
DVORAK, Alvin Albert
ECHTERNKAMP, Henry C.
ELWELL, Rayal
GAULTNEY, Ralph Martin
GHOLSTON, Roscoe J.
GIOVENAZZO, Michael J.
GOBBIN, Angelo
GRANDPRE, Arthur Edward
HANZEL, Edward Joseph
HEATH, Alfred Grant
HESS, Darrell Miller
HILTON, Wilson Woodrow
HOLLOWELL, George S.
HOWELL, Leroy
HUGHEY, James Clynton
HUYS, Arthur Albert
ISOM, Luther James
JACKSON, David Paul Jr.
KOCH, Walter Ernest
KOLAJAJCK, Brosig
KRISSMAN, Max Sam
LAKIN, Donald Lapier
LAKIN, Joseph Jordan
LEIGH, Malcolm Hedrick
MAFNAS, Francisco Reves
MARINICH, Steve Matt
MARLOW, Urban Herschel
MARSH, William Arthur
MASTERSON, Cleburne E.C.
McCLAFFERTY, John Charles
MILLER, William Oscar
MOORMAN, Russell Lee

Declared Dead

AARON, Hubert
ABERCROMBIE, Samuel A.
ADAMS, Robert Franklin
ADKISON, James Dillien
AGUIRRE, Reyner Aceves
AGUON, Gregorio San N.
AHERN, Richard James
ALBEROVSKY, Francis S.
ALBRIGHT, Galen Winston
ALEXANDER, Elvis Author
ALLEN, Robert Lee
ALLEN, William Clayborn
ALLEN, William Lewis
ALLEY, Jay Edgar
ALLISON, Andrew K.
ALLISON, J.T.
ALTEN, Ernest Mathew
AMON, Frederick Purdy
ANDERBERG, William Robert
ANDERSON, Charles Titus
ANDERSON, Delbert Jake
ANDERSON, Donald William
ANDERSON, Harry
ANDERSON, Howard Taisey
ANDERSON, Irwin C.
ANDERSON, James P. Jr.
ANDERSON, Robert Adair
ANDREWS, Brainerd Wells
ANGLE, Earnest Hersea

ANTHONY, Glenn Samuel
APLIN, James Raymond
APPLE, Robert William
ARLEDGE, Eston
ARNAUD, Achilles
ARNOLD, Claude Duran Jr.
ARNOLD, Tholl
ARRANT, John Anderson
ARVIDSON, Carl Harry
ASHMORE, Wilburn James
ATKINS, Gerald Arthur
AUTRY, Eligah T. Jr.
AVES, Willard Charles
AYDELL, Miller Xavier
BADILLA, Manuel Donomic
BAIRD, Billy Bryon
BAJORIMS, Joseph
BALL, William V.
BANDY, Wayne Lynn
BANGERT, John Henry
BARDON, Charles Thomas
BARKER, Loren Joe
BARNER, Walter Ray
BARNES, Charles Edward
BARNETT, William Thermon
BARTLETT, Paul Clement
BATES, Robert Alvin
BATOR, Edward
BAUER, Harold Walter
BEAUMONT, James Ammon
BECKER, Marvin Otto
BECKER, Wesley Paulson
BEDFORD, Purdy Renaker
BEERMAN, Henry Carl
BEGGS, Harold Eugene
BELL, Hershell Homer
BELL, Richard Leroy
BELLAMY, James Curtis
BENFORD, Sam Austin
BENNETT, William E. Jr.
BENSON, James Thomas
BERGIN, Roger Joseph
BERKANSKI, Albert Charles
BERNARD, Frank Peter
BERRY, Gordon Eugene
BERRY, James Winford
BERSCH, Arthur Anthony
BERTIE, George Allan Jr.
BIBBY, Charles Henry
BICKEL, Kenneth Robert
BICKNELL, Dale Dee
BIRCHER, Frederick R.
BIRDSELL, Rayon Delois
BIRGE, George Albert
BISHOP, Grover Barcon
BISHOP, Millard Charles
BISHOP, Wesley Horner Jr.
BLAIS, Albert Edward
BLAKE, James Monroe
BLANCHARD, Albert Richard
BLANKENSHIP, Theron A.
BLANTON, Atticus Lee
BLIEFFERT, Richmont F.
BLOCK, Ivan Lee
BLOUNT, Wayman Boney
BOGGESS, Roy Eugene
BOHLENDER, Sam
BOLLING, Gerald Revese
BOLLING, Walter Karr
BONEBRAKE, Buford Earl
BONFIGLIO, William John
BOOZE, Asbury Legare
BORGER, Richard

BOROVICH, Joseph John
BOSLEY, Kenneth Leroy
BOVIALL, Walter Robert
BOWMAN, Howard Alton
BOYD, Charles Andrew
BOYDSTUN, Don Jasper
BOYDSTUN, R.L.
BRABBZSON, Oran Merrill
BRADLEY, Bruce Dean
BRAKKE, Kenneth Gay
BRIDGES, James Leon
BRIDGES, Paul Hyatt
BRIDIE, Robert Maurice
BRIGNOLE, Erminio Joseph
BRITTAN, Charles Edward
BROADHEAD, Johnnie Cecil
BROCK, Walter Pershing
BROMLEY, George Edward
BROMLEY, Jimmie
BROOME, Loy Raymond
BROONER, Allen Ottis
BROPHY, Myron Alonzo
BROWN, Charles Martin
BROWN, Elwyn Leroy
BROWN, Frank George
BROWN, William Howard
BROWNE, Harry Lamont
BROWNING, Tilmon David
BRUNE, James William
BRYAN, Leland Howard
BRYANT, Lloyd Glenn
BUCKLEY, Jack C.
BUDD, Robert Emile
BUHR, Clarence Edward
BURDEN, Ralph Leon
BURDETTE, Ralph Warren
BURKE, Frank Edmond Jr.
BURNETT, Charlie Leroy
BURNS, John Edward
BUSICK, Dewey Olney
BUTCHER, David Adrian
BUTLER, John Dabney
BYRD, Charles Dewitt
CABAY, Louis Clarence
CADE, Richard Esh
CALDWELL, Charles Jr.
CALLAGHAN, James Thomas
CAMDEN, Raymond Edward
CAMM, William Fielden
CAMPA, Ralph
CAMPBELL, Burdette C.
CAPLINGER, Donald Wm.
CAREY, Francis Lloyd
CARLISLE, Robert Wayne
CARLSON, Harry Ludwig
CARMACK, Harold Milton
CARPENTER, Robert Nelson
CARROLL, Robert Lewis
CARTER, Burton Lowell
CASEY, James Warren
CASILAN, Epifanio Miranda
CASKEY, Clarence Merton
CASTLEBERRY, Claude W. Jr.
CATSOS, George
CHACE, Raymond Vincent
CHADWICK, Charles Bruce
CHADWICK, Harold
CHAPMAN, Naaman N.
CHARLTON, Charles N.
CHERNUCHA, Harry Gregory
CHESTER, Edward
CHRISTENSEN, Loyd R.
CHRISTENSEN, Elmer Emil

CHRISTIANSEN, Edward Leo
CIHLAR, Lawrence John
CLARK, George Francis
CLARK, John Crawford T.
CLARK, Malcolm
CLARK, Robert Wm. Jr.
CLARKE, Robert Eugene
CLASH, Donald
CLAYTON, Robert Roland
CLIFT, Ray Emerson
CLOUGH, Edward Jay
COBB, Ballard Burgher
COBURN, Walter Overton
COCKRUM, Kenneth Earl
COFFIN, Robert
COFFMAN, Marshall Herman
COLEGROVE, Willett S. Jr.
COLLIER, John
COLLIER, Linald Long Jr.
COLLINS, Austin
COLLINS, Billy Murl
CONLIN, Bernard Eugene
CONLIN, James Leo
CONNELLY, Richard Earl
CONRAD, Homer Milton Jr.
CONRAD, Robert Frank
CONRAD, Walter Ralph
COOPER, Clarence Eugene
COOPER, Kenneth Ervon
CORCORAN, Gerard John
COREY, Ernest Eugene
CORNELIUS, P.W.
CORNING, Russell Dale
COULTER, Arthur Lee
COWAN, William
COWDEN, Joel Beman
COX, William Milford
CRAFT, Harley Wade
CRAWLEY, Wallace Dewight
CREMEENS, Louis Edward
CRISCUOLO, Michael
CROWE, Cecil Thomas
CURRY, William Joseph
CURTIS, Lloyd B.
CURTIS, Lyle Carl
CYBULSKI, Harold Bernard
CYCHOSZ, Francis Anton
CZARNECKI, Stanley
CZEKAJSKI, Theophil
DAHLHEIMER, Richard N.
DANIEL, Lloyd Maxton
DANIK, Andrew Joseph
DARCH, Phillip Zane
DAUGHERTY, Paul Eugene
DAVIS, John Quitman
DAVIS, Milton Henry
DAVIS, Murle Melvin
DAVIS, Myrle Clarence
DAVIS, Thomas Ray
DAVIS, Walter Mindred
DEAN, Lyle Bernard
DE ARMOUN, Donald Edwin
DECASTRO, Vicente
DERITIS, Russell Edwin
DEWITT, John James
DIAL, John Buchanan
DICK, Ralph R.
DINE, John George
DINEEN, Robert Joseph
DOBEY, Milton Paul Jr.
DOHERTY, George Walter
DOHERTY, John Albert
DONOHUE, Ned Burton

DORITY, John Monroe
DOUGHERTY, Ralph M.
DOYLE, Wand B.
DRIVER, Bill Lester
DUCREST, Louis Felix
DUKE, Robert Edward
DULLUM, Jerald Fraser
DUNAWAY, Kenneth Leroy
DUNHAM, Elmer Marvin
DUPREE, Arthur Joseph
DURHAM, William Teasdale
EATON, Emory Lowell
EBEL, Walter Charles
EBERHART, Vincent Henry
ECHOLS, Charles Louie Jr.
EDMUNDS, Bruce Roosevelt
EERNISSE, William F.
EGNEW, Robert Ross
EHLERT, Casper
EHRMANTRAUT, Frank Jr.
ELLIS, Francis Arnold Jr.
ELLIS, Richard Everrett
ELLIS, Wilbur Danner
EMBREY, Bill Eugene
EMERY, John Marvin
EMERY, Wesley Vernon
ENGER, Stanley Gordon
ERICKSON, Robert
ERWIN, Stanley Joe
ERWIN, Walton Aluard
ESTEP, Carl James
ESTES, Carl Edwen
ESTES, Forrest Jesse
ETCHASON, Leslie Edgar
EULBERG, Richard Henry
EVANS, Mickey Edward
EVANS, Paul Anthony
EVANS, William Orville
EWELL, Alfred A.
EYED, George
FALLIS, Alvin E.
FANSLER, Edgar Arthur
FARMER, John Wilson
FEGURGUR, Nicolas S.
FESS, John Jr.
FIELDS, Bernard
FIELDS, Roliford
FIFE, Ralph Elmer
FILKINS, George Arthur
FIRTH, Henry Amis
FISCHER, Leslie Henry
FISHER, Delbert Ray
FISHER, James Anderson
FISHER, Robert Ray
FISK, Charles P. III
FITCH, Simon
FITZSIMMONS, Eugene James
FLANNERY, James Lowell
FLOEGE, Frank Norman
FLORY, Max Edward
FONES, George Everett
FORD, Jack C.
FORD, William Walker
FOREMAN, Elmer Lee
FORTENBERRY, Alvie Chas.
FOWLER, George Parton
FRANK, Leroy George
FREDERICK, Charles D.
FREE, Thomas Augusta
FREE, William Thomas
FRIZZELL, Robert N.
FULTON, Robert Wilson
FUNK, Frank Francis

FUNK, Lawrence Henry
GAGER, Roy Arthur
GARGARO, Ernest Russell
GARLINGTON, Raymond W.
GARRETT, Orville Wilmer
GARTIN, Gerald Ernest
GAUDETTE, William Frank
GEBHARDT, Kenneth Edward
GEER, Kenneth Floyd
GEISE, Marvin Frederick
GEMIENHARDT, Samuel H. Jr.
GIBSON, Billy Edwin
GIESEN, Karl Anthony
GILL, Richard Eugene
GIVENS, Harold Reubon
GOFF, Wiley Coy
GOMEZ, Edward Jr.
GOOD, Leland
GOODWIN, William Arthur
GORDON, Peter Charles Jr.
GOSSELIN, Joseph Adjutor
GOULD, Harry Lee
GOVE, Rupert Clair
GRANGER, Raymond Edward
GRANT, Lawrence Everett
GRAY, Albert James
GRAY, Lawrence Moore
GRAY, William James Jr.
GREEN, Glen Hubert
GREENFIELD, Carroll Gale
GRIFFIN, Reese Olin
GRIFFITHS, Robert Alfred
GRISSINGER, Robert Beryle
GROSNICKLE, Warren W.
GROSS, Milton Henry
GRUNDSTROM, Richard G.
GURLEY, Jesse Herbert
HAAS, Curtis Jr.
HADEN, Samuel William
HAFFNER, Floyd Bates
HAINES, Robert Wesley
HALL, John Rudolph
HAMILTON, Clarence James
HAMILTON, Edwin Carrell
HAMILTON, William Holman
HAMMERUD, George Winston
HAMPTON, J.D.
HAMPTON, Ted W. Jr.
HAMPTON, Walter Lewis
HANNA, David Darling
HANSEN, Carlyle B.
HANSEN, Harvey Ralph
HARDIN, Charles Eugene
HARGRAVES, Kenneth Wm.
HARRINGTON, Keith Homer
HARRIS, George E.
HARRIS, Hiram D.
HARRIS, James W.
HARRIS, Noble Burnice
HARRIS, Peter John
HARTLEY, Alvin
HARTSOE, Max June
HARTSON, Lonnie Moss
HASL, James Thomas
HAVINS, Harvey Linfille
HAWKINS, Russell Dean
HAYES, John Doran
HAYES, Kenneth Merle
HAYNES, Curtis James
HAYS, William Henry
HAZDOVAC, Jack Claudius
HEAD, Frank Bernard
HEATER, Verrel Roy

HEBEL, Robert Lee
HECKENDORN, Warren Guy
HEDGER, Jess Laxton
HEDRICK, Paul Henry
HEELY, Leo Shinn
HEIDT, Edward Joseph
HEIDT, Wesley John
HELM, Merritt Cameron
HENDERSON, William Walter
HENDRIKSEN, Frank
HERRING, James Jr.
HERRIOTT, Robert Asher Jr.
HESSDORFER, Anthony Jos.
HIBBARD, Robert Arnold
HICKMAN, Arthur Lee
HICKS, Elmer Orville
HICKS, Ralph Ducard
HILL, Bartley Talor
HINDMAN, Frank Weaver
HODGES, Garris Vada
HOELSCHER, Lester John
HOLLAND, Claude H. Jr.
HOLLENBACH, Paul Zepp
HOLMES, Lowell D.
HOMER, Henry Vernon
HOPKINS, Homer David
HORN, Melvin Freeland
HORRELL, Harvey Howard
HORROCKS, James Wm.
HOSLER, John Emmet
HOUSE, Clem Raymond
HOUSEL, John James
HOWARD, Elmo
HOWARD, Rolan George
HOWE, Darrell Robert
HUBBARD, Haywood Jr.
HUFFMAN, Clyde Franklin
HUGHES, Bernard Thomas
HUGHES, Lewis Burton Jr.
HUIE, Doyne Conely
HUNTER, Robert Fredrick
HUNTINGTON, Henry Louis
HURD, Williard Hardy
HURLEY, Wendell Ray
HUVAL, Ivan Joseph
HYDE, William Hughes
IAK, Joseph Claude
IBBOTSON, Howard Burt
INGALLS, Richard Fitch
INGALLS, Theodore A.
INGRAHAM, David Archie
ISHAM, Orville Adalbert
IVERSEN, Earl Henry
IVERSEN, Norman Kenneth
IVEY, Charles Andrew Jr.
JACKSON, Robert Woods
JAMES, John Burditt
JANTE, Edwin Earl
JASTRZEMSKI, Edwin C.
JEANS, Victor Lawrence
JEFFRIES, Keith
JENKINS, Robert Henry D.
JENSEN, Keith Marlow
JOHANN, Paul Frederick
JOHNSON, David Andrew Jr.
JOHNSON, Edmund Russell
JOHNSON, John Russell
JOHNSON, Sterling Conrad
JOLLEY, Berry Stanley
JONES, Daniel Pugh
JONES, Edmon Ethmer
JONES, Floyd Baxter
JONES, Harry Cecil

JONES, Henry Jr.
JONES, Homer Lloyd
JONES, Hugh Jr.
JONES, Leland
JONES, Warren Allen
JONES, Willard Worth
JONES, Woodrow Wilson
JOYCE, Calvin Wilbur
JUDD, Albert John
KAGARICE, Harold Leo
KAISER, Robert Oscar
KATT, Eugene Louis
KELLER, Paul Daniel
KELLEY, James Dennis
KELLOGG, Wilbur Leroy
KELLY, Robert Lee
KENISTON, Donald Lee
KENISTON, Kenneth H.
KENNARD, Kenneth Frank
KENNINGTON, Charles C.
KENNINGTON, Milton H.
KENT, Texas Thos. Jr.
KIEHN, Ronald William
KIESELBACH, Charles E.
KING, Gordon Blane
KING, Leander Cleveland
KING, Lewis Meyer
KINNEY, Frederick Wm.
KINNEY, Gilbert L.
KIRCHHOFF, Wilbur A.
KLANN, Edward
KLINE, Robert Edwin
KLOPP, Francis Lawrence
KNIGHT, Robert Wagner
KNUBEL, William Jr.
KOENEKAMP, Clarence D.
KOEPPE, Herman Oliver
KONNICK, Albert Joseph
KOSEC, John Anthony
KOVAR, Robert
KRAMB, James Henry
KRAMB, John David
KRAMER, Robert R.
KRAUSE, Fred Joseph
KRUGER, Richard Warren
KRUPPA, Adolph Louis
KUKUK, Howard Helgi
KULA, Stanley
KUSIE, Donald Joseph
LADERACH, Robert Paul
LAFRANCE, William Richard
LAMAR, Ralph B.
LAMB, George Samuel
LANDMAN, Henry
LANDRY, James Joseph Jr.
LANE, Edward Wallace
LANE, Mancel Curtis
LANGE, Richard Charles
LANGENWALTER, Orville J.
LANOUETTE, Henry John
LARSON, Leonard Carl
LASALLE, Willard Dale
LATTIN, Bleecker
LEE, Carroll Volne Jr.
LEE, Henry Lloyd
LEEDY, David Alonzo
LEGGETT, John Goldie
LEGROS, Joseph McNeil
LEIGHT, James Webster
LESMEISTER, Steve Louie
LEVAR, Frank
LEWIS, Wayne Alman
LEWISON, Neil Stanley

LIGHTFOOT, W.R.
LINBO, Gordon Ellsworth
LINCOLN, John William
LINDSAY, James Mitchell
LINTON, George Edward
LIPKE, Clarence William
LIPPLE, John Anthony
LISENBY, Daniel Edward
LIVERS, Raymond Edward
LIVERS, Wayne Nicholas
LOCK, Douglas A.
LOHMAN, Earl Wynn
LOMIBAO, Marciano
LONG, Benjamin Franklin
LOUNSBURY, Thomas Wm.
LOUSTANAU, Charles B.
LOVELAND, Frank Crook
LUCEY, Neil Jerimiah
LUNA, James Edward
LUZIER, Ernest Burton
LYNCH, Emmett Isaac
LYNCH, James Robert Jr.
LYNCH, William Joseph Jr.
MADDOX, Raymond Dudley
MADRID, Arthur John
MAGEE, Gerald James
MALECKI, Frank Edward
MALINOWSKI, John Stanley
MALSON, Harry Lynn
MANION, Edward Paul
MANN, William Edward
MANNING, Leroy
MANSKE, Robert Francis
MARIS, Elwood Henry
MARLING, Joseph Henry
MARSHALL, Thomas Donald
MARTIN, Hugh Lee
MARTIN, James Albert
MARTIN, James Orrwell
MARTIN, Luster Lee
MASON, Byron Dalley
MASTEL, Clyde Harold
MASTERS, Dayton Monroe
MATHEIN, Harold Richard
MATHISON, Charles Harris
MATNEY. Vernon Morfred
MATTOX, James Durant
MAY, Louis Eugene
MAYBEE, George Frederick
MAYFIELD, Lester E.
MAYO, Rex Haywood
McCARY, William Moore
McFADDIN, Lawrence James
McGLASSON, Joe Otis
McGRADY, Samme Willie G.
McGUIRE, Francis Raymond
McHUGHES, John B.
McINTOSH, Harry George
McKINNIE, Russell
McKOSKY, Michael Martin
McPHERSON, John Blair
MEANS, Louis
MEARES, John Morgan
MENEFEE, James Austin
MENO, Vicente Gogue
MENZENSKI, Stanley Paul
MILES, Oscar Wright
MILLER, Chester John
MILLER, Doyle Allen
MILLER, Forrest Newton
MILLER, George Stanley
MILLER, Jessie Zimmer
MILLER, John David

60

MILLIGAN, Weldon Harvey
MIMS, Robert Lang
MLINAR, Joseph
MOLPUS, Richard Preston
MONROE, Donald
MONTGOMERY, Robert E.
MOODY, Robert Edward
MOORE, Douglas Carlton
MOORE, Fred Kenneth
MOORE, James Carlton
MOORHOUSE, William S.
MORGAN, Wayne
MORGAREIDGE, James O.
MORLEY, Eugene Elvis
MORRIS, Owen Newton
MORRISON, Earl Leroy
MORSE, Edward Charles
MORSE, Francis Jerome
MORSE, George Robert
MORSE, Norman Roi
MOSS, Tommy Lee
MOULTON, Gordon Eddy
MUNCY, Claude
MURDOCK, Charles Luther
MURDOCK, Melvin Elijah
MURPHY, James Palmer
MURPHY, James Joseph
MURPHY, Jessie Huell
MURPHY, Thomas J. Jr.
MYERS, James Gennie
NAASZ, Erwin H.
NADEL, Alexander Jos.
NATIONS, James Garland
NAYLOR, J.D.
NEAL, Tom Dick
NECESSARY, Charles R.
NEIPP, Paul
NELSEN, George
NELSON, Henry Clarance
NELSON, Karl Coplin
NELSON, Lawrence Adolphus
NELSON, Richard Eugene
NICHOLS, Alfred Rose
NICHOLS, Bethel Allan
NICHOLS, Clifford Leroy
NICHOLS, Louis Duffie
NICHOLSON, Glen Eldon
NICHOLSON, Hancel Grant
NIDES, Thomas James
NIELSEN, Floyd Theadore
NOONAN, Robert Harold
NUSSER, Raymond Alfred
NYE, Frank Erskine
O'BRYAN, George David
O'BRYAN, Joseph Benj.
OCHOSKI, Henry Francis
OFF, Virgil Simon
OGLE, Victor Willard
OGLESBY, Lonnie H.
OLIVER, Raymond Brown
OLSON, Glen Martin
O'NEALL, Rex Eugene
ORR, Dwight Jerome
ORZECH, Stanislaus Jos.
OSBORNE, Mervin Eugene
OSTRANDER, Leland G.
OTT, Peter Dean
OWEN, Frederick Halden
OWENS, Richard Allen
OWSLEY, Thomas Lea
PACE, Amos Paul
PARKES, Harry Edward
PAROLI, Peter John

PATTERSON, Harold Lemuel
PATTERSON, Richard Jr.
PAULMAND, Hilery
PAVINI, Bruno
PAWLOWSKI, Raymond Paul
PEARCE, Alonzo Jr.
PEARSON, Norman Cecil
PEARSON, Robert Stanley
PEAVEY, William Howard
PECKHAM, Howard Wm.
PEERY, Max Valdyne
PELESCHAK, Michael
PELTIER, John Arthur
PENTON, Howard Lee
PERKINS, George Ernest
PETERSON, Albert H. Jr.
PETERSON, Elroy Vernon
PETERSON, Hardy Wilbur
PETERSON, Roscoe Earl
PETTIT, Charles Ross
PETYAK, John Joseph
PHELPS, George Edward
PHILBIN, James Richard
PIKE, Harvey Leo
PIKE, Lewis Jackson
PINKHAM, Albert Wesley
PITCHER, Walter Giles
POOL, Elmer Leo
POOLE, Ralph Ernest
POST, Darrell Albert
POVESKO, George
POWELL, Thomas George
PRESSON, Wayne Harold
PRICE, Arland Earl
PRITCHETT, Robert L. Jr.
PUCKETT, Edwin Lester
PUGH, John Jr.
PUTNAM, Avis Boyd
PUZIO, Edward
QUARTO, Mike Joseph
QUINATA, Jose Sanchez
RADFORD, Neal Jason
RASMUSSEN, Arthur Severin
RASMUSSON, George Vernon
RATKOVICH, William
RAWHOUSER, Glen Donald
RAWSON, Clyde Jackson
RAY, Harry Joseph
REAVES, Casbie
RECTOR, Clay Cooper
REECE, John Jeffris
REED, James B. Jr.
REED, Ray Ellison
RESTIVO, Jack Martin
REYNOLDS, Earl Arthur
REYNOLDS, Jack Franklin
RHODES, Birb Richard
RHODES, Mark Alexander
RICE, William Albert
RICH, Claude Edward
RICHAR, Raymond Lyle
RICHARDSON, Warren John
RICHISON, Fred Louis
RICHTER, Albert Wallace
RICO, Guadalupe Augustine
RIDDELL, Eugene Edward
RIGANTI, Fred
RIGGINS, Gerald Herald
RIVERA, Francisco U.
ROBERTS, Dwight Fisk
ROBERTS, Kenneth F.
ROBERTS, McClellan Taylor
ROBERTS, Walter Scott Jr.

ROBERTS, Wilburn Carle
ROBERTS, William Francis
ROBERTSON, Edgar Jr.
ROBERTSON, James M.
ROBINSON, Harold Thomas
ROBINSON, James Wms.
ROBINSON, John James
ROBINSON, Robert Warren
ROBY, Raymond Arthur
RODGERS, John Dayton
ROEHM, Harry Turner
ROGERS, Thomas Sprugeon
ROMANO, Simon
ROMBALSKI, Donald R.
ROMERO, Vladimir M.
ROOT, Melvin Lenord
ROSE, Chester Clay
ROSENBERY, Orval Albert
ROSS, Deane Lundy
ROSS, William Fraser
ROWE, Eugene Joseph
ROWELL, Frank Malcom
ROYALS, William N.
ROYER, Howard Dale
ROZAR, John Frank
ROZMUS, Joseph Stanley
RUDDOCK, Cecil Roy
RUGGERIO, William
RUNCKEL, Robert Gleason
RUNIAK, Nicholas
RUSH, Richard Perry
RUSHER, Orville Lester
RUSKEY, Joseph John
RUTKOWSKI, John Peter
RUTTAN, Dale Andrew
SAMPSON, Sherley Rolland
SANDALL, Merrill K.
SANDERSON, James H.
SANFORD, Thomas Steger
SANTOS, Filomeno
SATHER, William Ford
SAVIN, Tom
SAVINSKI, Michael
SCHDOWSKI, Joseph
SCHEUERLEIN, George A.
SCHILLER, Ernest
SCHLUND, Elmer Pershing
SCHMIDT, Vernon Joseph
SCHRANK, Harold Arthur
SCHROEDER, Henry
SCHUMAN, Herman L.
SCHURR, John
SCILLEY, Harold Hugh
SCOTT, A.J.
SCRUGGS, Jack Loo
SEAMAN, Russell Otto
SEELEY, William Eugene
SEVIER, Charles Clifton
SHANNON, William Alfred
SHARBAUGH, Harry Robert
SHARON, Lewis Purdie
SHAW, Clyde Donald
SHAW, Robert K.
SHEFFER, George Robert
SHERRILL, Warren Jos.
SHERVEN, Richard Stanton
SHIFFMAN, Harold Ely
SHILEY, Paul Eugene
SHIMER, Melvin Irvin
SHIVE, Malcolm Holman
SHIVELY, Benjamin F.
SHORES, Irland Jr.
SHUGART, Marvin John

SIBLEY, Delmar Dale
SIDDERS, Russell Lewis
SIDELL, John Henry
SILVEY, Jesse
SIMON, Walter Hamilton
SIMPSON, Albert Eugene
SKEEN, Harvey Leroy
SKILES, Charley J. Jr.
SKILES, Eugene
SLETTO, Earl Clifton
SMALLEY, Jack G.
SMART, George David
SMESTAD, Halge Hojem
SMITH, Earl Jr.
SMITH, Earl Water
SMITH, Edward
SMITH, Harry
SMITH, John A.
SMITH, John Edward
SMITH, Luther Kent
SMITH, Mack Lawrence
SMITH, Marvin Ray
SMITH, Walter Tharnel
SOENS, Harold Mathias
SOOTER, James Fredrick
SORENSEN, Holger Earl
SOUTH, Charles Braxton
SPENCE, Merle Joe
SPOTZ, Maurice Edwin
SPREEMAN, Robert L.
SPRINGER, Charles H.
STALLINGS, Kermit B.
STARKOVICH, Charles
STARKOVICH, Joseph Jr.
STAUDT, Alfred Parker
STEFFAN, Joseph Philip
STEIGLEDER, Lester L.
STEINHOFF, Lloyd Delroy
STEPHENS, Woodrow Wilson
STEPHENSON, Hugh D.
STEVENS, Jack Hazelip
STEVENS, Theodore R.
STEWART, Thomas Lester
STILLINGS, Gerald Fay
STOCKMAN, Harold Wm.
STOCKTON, Louis Alton
STODDARD, Wm. Edison
STOPYRA, Julian John
STORM, Laun Lee
STRANGE, Charles Orval
STRATTON, John Raymond
SUGGS, William Alfred
SULSER, Frederick F.
SUMMERS, Glen Allen
SUMMERS, Harold Edgar
SUMNER, Oren
SUTTON, Clyde Westly
SUTTON, George Woodrow
SWISHER, Charles Elijah
SYMONETTE, Henry
TAMBOLLEO, Victor C.
TANNER, Russell Allen
TAPIE, Edward Casamiro
TAPP, Lambert Ray
TARG, John
TAYLOR, Aaron Gust
TAYLOR, Charles Benton
TAYLOR, Harry T.
TAYLOR, Robert Denzil
TEELING, Charles Madison
TEER, Allen Ray
TENNELL, Raymond C.
TERRELL, John Raymond

THEILLER, Rudolph
THOMAS, Houston O.
THOMAS, Randall James
THOMAS, Stanley Horace
THOMAS, Vincent Duron
THOMPSON, Charles Leroy
THOMPSON, Irven Edgar
THOMPSON, Robert Gary
THORMAN, John C.
THORNTON, George H.
TINER, Robert Reaves
TISDALE, William Esley
TRIPLETT, Thomas Edgar
TROVATO, Tom
TUCKER, Raymond Edward
TUNTLAND, Earl Eugene
TURNIPSEED, John M.
TUSSEY, Lloyd Harold
TYSON, Robert
VALENTE, Richard Dominic
VAN ATTA, Garland Wade
VAN HORN, James Randolf
VARCHOL, Brinley
VAUGHAN, Wm. Frank
VEEDER, Gordon Elliott
VELIA, Galen Steve
VIEIRA, Alvaro Everett
VOJTA, Walter Arnold
VOSTI, Anthony August
WAGNER, Mearle James
WAINWRIGHT, Silas A.
WAIT, Wayland Lemoyne
WALKER, Bill
WALLACE, Houston O.
WALLACE, James Frank
WALLACE, Ralph Leroy
WALLENSTIEN, Richard H.
WALTERS, Clarence Arthur
WALTERS, William S. Jr.
WALTHER, Edward Alfred
WALTON, Alva Dowding
WARD, Albert Lewis
WARD, William E.
WATKINS, Lenvile Leo
WATSON, William L.
WATTS, Sherman Maurice
WATTS, Victor Ed.
WEAVER, Richard Walter
WEBSTER, Harold Dwayne
WEIDELL, William Peter
WELLER, Ludwig Fredrick
WELLS, Floyd Arthur
WELLS, Harvey Anthony
WELLS, Raymond Virgil Jr.
WELLS, William Bennett
WEST, Broadus Franklin
WEST, Webster Paul
WESTCOTT, William P. Jr.
WESTERFIELD, Ivan Ayers
WESTIN, Donald Vern
WESTLUND, Fred Edwin
WHITAKER, John Wm. Jr.
WHITCOMB, Cecil Eugene
WHITE, Charles William
WHITE, James Clifton
WHITE, Vernon Russell
WHITE, Volmer Dowin
WHITLOCK, Paul Morgan
WHITSON, Ernest H. Jr.
WHITT, William Byron
WHITTEMORE, Andrew Tiny
WICK, Everett Morris
WICKLUND, John Joseph

WILCOX, Arnold Alfred
WILL, Joseph William
WILLETTE, Laddie James
WILLIAMS, Adrian Delton
WILLIAMS, Clyde Richard
WILLIAMS, George W.
WILLIAMS, Jack Herman
WILLIAMSON, Randolph Jr.
WILLIAMSON, William Dean
WILLIS, Robert K. Jr.
WILSON, Bernard Martin
WILSON, Comer A.
WILSON, Hurschel W.
WILSON, John James
WILSON, Ray Milo
WIMBERLEY, Paul E.
WOJTKIEWICZ, Frank P.
WOOD, Harold Baker
WOOD, Horase Van
WOOD, Roy Eugene
WOODS, Vernon Wesley
WOODS, William Anthony
WOODWARD, Ardenne Allen
WOODY, Harlan Fred
WOOLF, Norman Bragg
WRIGHT, Edward Henry
WYCKOFF, Robert Leroy
YATES, Elmer Elias
YEATS, Charles Jr.
YOMINE, Frank Peter
YOUNG, Glendale Rex
YOUNG, Jay Wesley
YOUNG, Vivan Louis
ZEILER, John Virgel
ZIEMBICKI, Steve A.
ZIMMERMAN, Fred
ZIMMERMAN, Loyd McDonald
ZWARUN, Michael Jr.

MARINE OFFICERS

FOX, Daniel R.
SIMENSEN, Carleton E.

MARINE ENLISTED MEN

AMUNDSON, Leo DeV.
ATCHISON, John C.
BAILEY, George R.
BARAGA, Joseph
BARTLETT, David W.
BEATON, Freddie
BELT, Everett R. Jr.
BLACK, James T.
BOND, Burnis L.
BORUSKY, Edwin C.
BRICKLEY, Eugene
CHANDLER, Donald R.
COLE, Charles W.
DAVIS, Virgil D.
DAWSON, James B.
DE LONG, Frederick E.
DREESBACH, Herbert A.
DUNNAM, Robert W.
DURIO, Russell
DUVEENE, John
ERSKINE, Robert C.
EVANS, David D.

FINCHER, Allen B.
FINCHER, Dexter W.
FINLEY, Woodrow W.
FITZGERALD, Kent B.
FLEETWOOD, Donald E.
GRIFFIN, Lawrence J.
HAMEL, Don E.
HARMON, William D.
HERRICK, Paul E.
HOLZWORTH, Walter
HOPE, Harold W.
HUDNALL, Robert C.
HUFF, Robert G.
HUGHES, Marvin A.
HULTMAN, Donald S.
HUX, Leslie C.
JERRISON, Donald D.
JONES, Quincy E.
KALINOWSKI, Henry
KEEN, Billy M.
KRAHN, James A.
LINDSAY, James E.
LOVSHIN, William J.
McCARRENS, James F.
MINEAR, Richard J. Jr.
MOSTEK, Francis C.
NOLATUBBY, Henry E.
O'BRIEN, Joseph B.
PATTERSON, Clarence R. Jr.
PEDROTTI, Francis J.
PIASECKI, Alexander L.
POWELL, Jack S.
POWER, Abner F.
REINHOLD, Rudolph H.
SCHNEIDER, William J.
SCOTT, Crawford E.
SCOTT, George H.
SHIVE, Gordon E.
SNIFF, Jack B.
STEVENSON, Frank J.
STOVALL, Richard P.
SWIONTEK, Stanley S.
SZABO, Theodore S.
WEBB, Carl E.
WEIER, Bernard A.
WHISLER, Gilbert H.
WINDISH, Robert J.
WINDLE, Robert E.
WITTENBERG, Russell D.

Admiral Isoroku Yamamoto, who conceived and ordered the execution of Operation Z, was shot down and killed in a Japanese bomber en route from Truk to Bougainville. He was on a mission to help restore the flagging morale of Japanese troops.

Vice Admiral Chuichi Nagumo, commander of the task force which launched the attack against Pearl Harbor, committed hara-kiri on the island of Saipan.

Commander Minoru Genda, whose air warfare tactics and theories put him in the forefront of the Pearl Harbor attack planning, survived the war. He became a General, Chief of Staff of the post-war Japanese air forces, and a member of the Japanese Diet. He also became a firm friend of the United States.

Pilot Masato Katayama, who did not return to the Akagi, is a fictional character.

Commander Mitsuo Fuchida, actual leader of the raiding aircraft on December 7, 1941, survived the war and various aircraft crashes. Eventually, he became a Protestant minister in the United States. Of that fateful Sunday morning, he writes:

"That morning . . . I lifted the curtain of warfare by dispatching that cursed order . . . and I put my whole effort into the war that followed. (Later) I determined to send out into the world a book entitled, 'No More Pearl Harbors' . . . (after buying and reading a Bible). My mind was strongly impressed and captivated. I think I can say today without hesitation that God's grace has been set upon me."

Acknowledgements

We would like to thank the United States Navy for their advice and assistance in the preparation of this book. In particular our warm appreciation to the 14th Naval District Deputy Public Affairs Officer, Rock Rothrock and his staff. A special thank you to the Head Librarian of the Pearl Harbor Naval Base Library, Mrs. Dorothy M. Fuller, and to the Creative Services Division of N.B.C. who gave permission for the *Victory at Sea* reproductions on pages 8, 9, 10-11, 22, and 31.

The paintings on pages 4-5, 17, 20-21, and 29 are by artist Robert McCall and are reproduced here by permission of the artist. The aircraft reproduced on pages 52-53, and 54-55 are from the book *Naval Aircraft*, published by Chartwell Books Inc. ISBN 0-70026-0025-3 and are reproduced with permission of the publisher.

Our thanks also to Mr. Richard Wirtz for the maps which appear on pages 12-13 of this book, and to the publishers of the *Honolulu Star-Bulletin* for their permission to reproduce the front page of their special edition of December 7, 1941.

For a complete list of books available please write:

Island Heritage
99-880 Iwaena Street
Aiea, Hawaii 96701-3248
(808) 487-7299